Theory of Orange

Winner of the 2005-06 Transcontinental Poetry Award

THEORY OF ORANGE

RACHEL M. SIMON

PAVEMENT SAW PRESS
OHIO

Editor & Layout: David Baratier
Associate Editor: Sean Karns
Duck Logo: Joe Napora
Cover Art: Michael Branca (www.mikebranca.com)
Author Photo: Mary Schwalm

The author would like to thank the following people and places for helping in the process of putting together this manuscript: Karen Schechner, The Breadloaf Writers Conference, Billy Collins, Bridget Cross, Peter Harris, Tony Hoagland, Zdena Heller, Kate Knapp Johnson, Joan Larkin, Jan Heller Levi, Ken Hart, Marie Howe, Jill Huntsberger, Christopher Marks, Greg Nicholl, Tara J. Pearson, Ira Sadoff, Sarah Lawrence College, Diane Schechner, Adam Simon, Eileen Simon, Harvey Simon, Jason Stipp, Mark Wunderlich, The Vermont Studio Center, and Dean Young.

Pavement Saw Press
PO Box 6291
Columbus, OH 43206
pavementsaw.org

Products are available through the publisher or through:
SPD / 1341 Seventh St. / Berkeley, CA 94710 / 800.869.7553

Winner of the 2005-06 Transcontinental Poetry Award for an outstanding first book-length collection of poetry or prose. We read yearly from June 1st until August 15th. Send SASE for information.

Pavement Saw Press is a not for profit corporation, any donations are greatly appreciated and are considered as charitable tax donations under section 501(c) of the federal tax code.
Paper Trade: ISBN 978-1-886350-45-8

Contents

In Memory of
Seth Harris Mirsky
1976-1997

I'll make you a deal. I'll become a writer if you will.

Recipe for Success

Take a dollop of eighth-grade embarrassment
burn it in your cheeks for when doors
swing toward you faster than your arms can brace.
Befriend lost children in the produce.
Pitch your voice two feathers louder
than the hush of meeting your girlfriend's
older brother. Never break plates.
Once plates are smashed consider
creating a mosaic. Keep broken glass
in a paper bag for two years.
Upon packing for a new apartment
discover bag of glass and discard.
Situate yourself in a seat corresponding
to your desired birth order.
Consider what a cape
might do for your aesthetic. Return cape
to store clothing rack. Mix it,
mix it good. Dispose of any mementos
in your memento box to which
the associated memory does not evoke
instant boils. Phone some cousins,
compare childhoods, lose touch.

On Reading Something Life-changing During an Unimportant Plane Trip

Sitting next to someone balancing a spreadsheet
I am sifting through the day's omens:
the unkempt skunk, overhearing a truly sincere
declaration of love, a cloud
shaped like broccoli, a dream about your tooth.
I am reading a pass-the-time book,
something unassuming at thirty thousand feet.
I am 5′5″ and fit just fine in the middle seat
dancing the dance of the shared armrest,
tempted to tell only lies to my seatmates
here in row 19. A row without families
or crying babies, a row with a spreadsheet,
five noses, two portholes, and the final page
I will read today. We are cloud-shrouded.
I can't see Nebraska's grid.
I'm surprised by so many
cowboy boots on the flight.
I have broken a sweat from the page.
I no longer fit so comfortably
in the middle seat with my newfound
revelation and disregard for time zones.
My brain is writing subtitles at a very fast rate
and my pulse is indicating a certain love
of language, and the page, and a brunette
back home. I consider the landing gear. I consider
meals in brown bags and places a bufflehead
can find camouflage and places people
can find companionship and the pet rabbit
in the cat bag four rows ahead of me
on its first trip to Louisville.
We may all fall in love with horses.
The attendant offers me a small salty bag
but no insight or clasping of any kind.
No fiddlehead fern, finch, nostril
bucket, bullet, barge.

That about Which We Cannot Speak

Vijay tells a roomfull of poets
he's impatient for his parents to die
so he can write his memoir with details
undisputed by scientific fact or tinkering
shared in small-talk-cheese-eating moments.
Now he's just doing the dishes with one eye on the clock.

The rules in his kitchen are different than mine.
Out his window are the walls
Brooklyn built around whole families in small boxes. Out ours
twelve varieties of cement hold the flattest earth to its axle.
A child's plastic shovel strikes limestone bedrock.
Protective layers: pliable, unremitting.

Genealogy may include fashion expectation, more likely middle names.
If you can subvert the dominant paradigm for a few seconds,
I might lift this shelf right off the ground.
Somewhere in an old book there's treasure.
In the family there are secrets,
typically radiating out from a stark pubescence.

What if the world gets big again?
What if perspective can only be gained
standing on a mountaintop lazy susan spun by the lag of the earth.

Improvisation

One thing about human nature is that nobody
wants to know the exact dimensions of their small talk.
I can't imagine good advice.
If every human being has skin
how come I can see all of your veins?
Clicks and drips target my skull.
Important voices miss their target.
Some cities are ill suited for feet.
I'd never buy a door smaller than a tuba, you never know
what sort of friends you'll make.
In the future there will be less to remember.
In the past I have only my body and shoes.
The gut and throat are two entirely different animals.
My hands don't make good shoelaces, but I'm going to stay
in this lane, even if it's slower.
The trick was done with saltwater and smoke
and an ingredient you can only find in an
out-of-business ethnic food store.
It all comes down to hand-eye coordination.
Once it took all my energy to get you out of the tub
we had converted from an indoor pool to a house.
I ended up on snorkeling spam lists inadvertently.
It is all inadvertent.
If you don't believe me ask your mom.

Early Correspondence

I am uncovering your childhood nicknames
and sibling injury in the first livingroom
where you control the heat.
We are comparing Hebrew school stories
that smell of rejection
and long-haired college days.
The smattering of pungent romances
and the monotonous Iowa landscape
that brought you back to this city.
We are taking turns interrupting each other,
letting the conversation-baton slide
between our fingers,
exploring this newness, this room.

I am memorizing your chin's crease
and want to hold you by the elbows
or waist or by your words for a few moments more.
These are the getting-to-know-you games,
the first charcoal lines of a friendship,
a moment of your profile, all seven syllables
of your middle name. Now, you sign notes
simply: g.

Condor Man

I'll be plain.
During those summers
I joined approximately one hundred and twenty
juvenile diabetics in a baseball field
flailing our arms to signal Condor Man
to drop his bale of sugar free Chewels.

It sounds ridiculous.

Those summers I cheered babies
who gave themselves injections
for the first time. I ate government cheese.
The girl on the bunk above me had boobs
like empty toilet paper rolls. The oldest doctor's wife
took a midnight hike of senility through the woods
and helicopters flew in to find her.
Medical lectures taught us our huge babies would hurt,
how to read with Vaseline glasses, and to eat bread before beer.
They never mentioned heroin and a redhead from our bunk
overdosed in high school. We picked a tree
next to the soccer field to serenade.
Valerie sat her bare ass on the sink
to shave her legs and married our best friend
four years later. Big Joe slept with
the tiny aerobics instructor from Mexico
in the laundry room, in a canoe, even the campers knew.

I can't believe I'm writing another
about summer camp.

We screamed into industrial fans.
We met the cerebral palsic.
I was not alone.

Today we are a veterinarian,
a professor, and an IRS mom.
Today we are at Manhattan restaurants

telling scar-tissue stories
churning the stomachs of our peers
in fields near southern Oklahoma
and on the camp's LiveCam we're still
watching for Condor Man in the sky.

EDIBLES

One must have imagination
in the kitchen, and a wooden bowl
large enough to layer every element
of pleasure. Those ingredients
are not only garlic and butter.
Some are seasonal and cannot be found
in retirement communities.
The residents remember when gluttony
was a sin. Do not ask them
to dirty their hands.

The only important etiquette guideline
is to put your napkin on your lap.
Controlling the amount of food
that actually makes it into the mouth
can be the responsibility
of your dining companions.
If there is no serviette available,
use the right shoulder portion
of your shirt. Dining shirtless
is strongly discouraged.

The impatient burn their tongues
at every hot meal as the honorable mention
ribbons are distributed for the
allergic, picky, and clean plate club.
Countertops should be kept clear of
these indulgent awards.
Formica formica. For my portion
omit all traces of onion.
For your complexion—
cucumbers over the eye.

The gratification of home cooking
ends with a bulldozer.
Unbroken dishes and
indecipherable paprakash recipes

may be passed down to youngsters
uninterested in any nostalgia
lacking a self starring role.
Do not chop them into a sauce of the ungrateful.
Nobody likes the flavor.

Not Another Lake Poem

My father proposed in his backyard.
The yard where my twin cousins split my head
and my Zadie grew delicate tomatoes.
I imagine my mother wearing some sixties sweater
and the proudest possible grin.
Now we covet her glow-orange mumu
that makes for a last minute Halloween costume
with rolling pin and shower cap.
My parents were reared in Cleveland—
before the lake was tested,
found overly hospitable to danger,
and locked up with a sign that said
this lake is dangerous children,
go sit in the icebox—
We have actual noses.
We worry when the blank line
asks our weight in consideration
of the horse we will mount.
My grandmother's dowry was supposed to be
a cow and horse, but, depending on the translation,
all Zadie got was the tail.
I have a collection of textures,
shoeboxes full of smells,
libraries of insecurities,
and three handsewn quilts.

On Giving a Presentation in the Bible Belt on Interracial Lesbian Couples in Film

It counted as forty percent of my grade
and I drove my tiny red car that scraped the ground
to four different video stores in two different counties
to find the most revealing tapes.

My thesis was that it is always a bigger deal
that the couples are queer than interracial
there is a mother screaming *it's a girl*
it's a girl and never a skin color issue.

More than one Christian fundamentalist student
carried a non-miniature version of the bible to class,
but only one took it out and flattened her palm
on the page that speaks to homosexual abomination.

Those years I carried a small lime green book
with a black elastic band in my backpack.
Occasionally I would draw sketches of a tree trunk
splitting or an uninteresting lecturer's ear.

I wrote small poems on unlined pages
about being misunderstood or elated
or the way the wind sounds in my treeless Texas
settling for a slope instead of a hill.

Insurrection

You wake up in bed with Stanley Kunitz and all of his ninety-nine years, unaware if you've bedded your first laureate or if Electra has conquered the rest of your subconscious—she orders your homunculi to poke the sharp end of their picket signs into the wet inside of your skin. They're campaigning for the labor union your therapist put out of business, whose office window overlooks the city's steeples. Fifty minutes of watching clouds wisp, roll, and disintegrate from a couch that has only two cushions. This indicates a *loveseat*, but the Hippocratic oath forbids it. However, the dreams you're having, your hand caught lazily in the therapist's curly hair, should not be alarming. In the dreams where you're nuzzling Stanley's chest his pajamas are soft from years of washing and young writers' faces rolling through the night.

Names of the Hurricanes

In 2008 I will plow through the Pacific—
a whirlwind. The ocean will empty into my storm
and crash around the bowl of whales
left behind. I will wrap my storm-arms
so the inside of my elbows crush mountains
and the wet-hair feeling overwhelms.
The sky will remain citrus, contrary to the mud
sucked up and poured down the sides of anything
vertical. Chocolate town.
The next storm the size of a family
who survives: large, loud, schmaltz
hard at the top of the soup. Exaggerating
margins, exaggerating everything,
exaggerating Lake Erie's proximity
to the eye of the storm. Looking out
a round eye. Swirling brown through
all the blues. Picking up every baby,
tossing her into the air, eliciting joy
on the circular path. Full fidelity
to every drop, every grain,
every time the phone rings three times
and we raise our eyes to look at it.
Suspicious in a way suspicion
has never been embodied.
Strong in a way that makes you
simultaneously frozen in place
and fleeing to find a new home,
new life, new pair of sandals.
Ones that won't rub your baby toe raw
after only one season of migration.
Slowing over land. Losing the power
promised by the water. Going to Canada,
rolling over in the bed,
sliding the peg of the reading lamp
to the off position.

Knotty

The whole houseful of women,
menopausal and clenched,
didn't notice
the day the doorbell stopped ringing,

wearing gauzy white dresses
to cover the brittle angles
growing beneath, peppermint lotion
to soothe hot temples,

synchronized swimming
through their morning routine,
a stormfront of elbows—sharp to the world,
held steady halfway to the cereal bowl,

surrounded by contortionist oak trees
they gather extra-arthritic messages
from the bark to strengthen their hands,
now, no longer as vulnerable.

Wolcott Avenue

I could see my breath from underneath
the seven-blanket winter
in our first Chicago apartment
with its woosh of radiators we didn't control.

I looked all the time at your face
the angles of a meticulously trimmed beard
nostrils big enough to fit my thumbs.
The noisiest mice possible lived in those walls.

All the furniture and most of our utensils
from people moved into nursing homes,
except for the dresser, bought
at the convent going-out-of-business sale.

We cleaned the kitchen together and melded
the styles of my mother and your single father,
compromised on sandwich bags, chili recipes,
and a couple's crush on a mutual friend.

Or maybe, we never compromised at all:
I omitted the cumin from the pot,
decided which holidays we would celebrate,
and annihilated your healthy eating habits.

You rubbed my cold feet and learned to smile
though your head ached at the world's loudest
polka concert, gave up on an athletic dream,
and relearned how to fry hot dogs.

It was an exercise in selfish and selfless
with the exception of that one frisbee game,
on the beach closest to Wolcott Avenue
where we never shared a peeled mango on a stick.

When You're Not Allowed to Daydream

One can live for years not knowing the teaspoon is inaccurate. Call the bureau of weights and measures. They'll understand. In massage school I learned to rub a full belly in a clockwise motion to aid in digestion. In the theory of orange, what is the best way to skin a grape? The citrus board feels strongly about the marketing campaign's mouth sores. Cracking a stranger's knuckles will not necessarily lead to mold under the nails. A Yogi can get away with that posture. I know to slouch is not the answer, yet all these crazy and abusive men never have a shortage of wives. No, I never could touch my toes. The irony doesn't end there. I kill bugs with my palm. If I had that many legs I wouldn't waste my time on some mediocre ceiling. When I fly I never dress for the occasion. When I land you can appreciate the thud. Just keep running, the parasail will take care of you. If the wind deposits you in a gift shop it is only appropriate to buy one moderately priced tchotchke.

Anxiety

I've turned in this niche so many times,
I've worn the edges smooth around me.
The curves of my shoulders and hips
fit into this space, fat pupils fill the dark.

Soon I'll take the empty boxes down
and fill them again, trying
to discard all I have
that ties me to modest trinkets

of my past perfect lives. I'm not ready
to throw myself upward, disembark
on my ripe wings,
yank the grapnel above my head.

I'll dress up in the costumes of a new body
learn to roll around until the bend of my neck
fits, like all those who came before and left before
and dug their nails into the floorboards.

&

Explosions are best well planned.
Hat in hand, no man, no man, not even me.

Nixzmary

Nixzmary, Nizmary, Nixmarie, your name a lamentation
for an ill-mannered metropolis.
A name we'd praise as evidence of the imaginative.
A name we'd like untethered from its chooser,
the receiver black both eyes
before succumbing to unimaginable inaction—
vapor until its boots meet your noseteeth.
A puzzle in which you must make new words from the letters "mother."
I cannot fill the space around the chapel with unimaginable.
I look at the pictures of twine and chair chanting
tetherball, tetherball, tetherball to her heartbeat.
Police remove small furniture and the girl the weight of a four year old.
Every mother.

ILLNESS, ILLINOIS

Its hardscrabble furlongs pull toward
unfathomable electricity.

Veins? No. Thank you.

Jaywalking momentum floats a piece of fuzz
from a sweater of someone long dead.

No pagoda.
Never.

Tactile Unearthing in a Warm Winter

I spent some time in the quiet morning
it wasn't like my life at all.

The only rhythm came from the underthuds
pumping to my wrists and sternum.

The nerves are dull in the place
where my jaw begins to be my ear,

more aware of my finger's sensation
than my face feeling.

There was no colored light show,
the usual big smiles were tight-lipped.

The entire membrane dull—
a constant hint of perspiration.

Precipitation

The skies always deliver at family funerals,
rain for the young and snow for the old.
There must've been a hundred people

at the graveside service, unprotected from the rain
standing on the California hillside. The orthodox pine box
shaped like a kid who loved basketball, six feet tall, so very thin.

They reserved a chair for Lea, in her mid-eighties,
at her grandson's funeral, to those close enough
she looked stoic—like her usual self.

Back at the house, over whitefish salad,
discussion of how the war toughened her,
the different ways each generation mourns.

Five years later, at Lea's funeral, the rabbi instructs
both her sons to remove their ties, hands them each
black, nearly plastic neckties he will cut

with his tiny rabbinical pocket knife
to symbolize mourning. The black sheep
comes out of hiding to send a condolence email;

we must be a family of writers. A generation of immigrants
working hard to send children into academic lives,
one writer dead at age 20, without leaving a note.

When the Radiator Is On I Dream of Funerals

An alternate version of yours
came to me—sleeping below
the poster-sized picture of you,
standing by a changing table
in your movie star stance,
you are legendary, 1953.

A happy family gathering,
not like your real funeral.
Relatives who survived the pogroms
arrive with pastel colored
leather briefcases, two hundred—
to pass out as party favors.

The kids hid from everyone
in the generation now beginning to die.
They jumped on the childhood bed
of a grown-up cousin,
the mountain of winter coats
splayed on the floor.

In a Season of Non-natural Disasters

In the compendium of trust
you'll not find a basket of woven fingers
or even invincible rebar
to support buckling knees.
It is un-alphabetized.
Its cupboard sorted by pungence—
smell of a crush's Ivory shampoo
on the school bus in the three short blocks
between your childhood front doors.

The compendium is never bland or nameless.
Mine has ruby depression glass
and my grandfather's trick of forgetting
English when blame comes around.
Neither bitter or embittered
non-eponymous but partially self-referential.
The way I speak to my brother's best friend
on the phone and forget which I'm talking to.

Rope

I can't picture you opening the door of a hardware store
comparison shopping rope gauge, fingering
the textures, picking the blend that felt best rolled in your fist.

Sometimes I think of you using a phone cord
for convenience, making your plan
while twisting its plastic coils around one long finger.

Friends attach oragami swans
to ceilings with thin twine
a short jog from the undergrad library.

Mom's hand absentmindedly traced the spine of her book
as the ambulance rolled past her window, no siren
to catch her eye, she lowered her head back to the page.

Five weeks later, Dad used his belt for a tourniquet,
unable to seal the hole left by the garden shears,
trying to descend the ladder with one hand.

You're there when he aches to tie his shoe,
when the doctors explain the robust progress
of all his wounds. Two years later,

two years in which I've pressed my face
into a pillowcase every night
I'm told you used a bedsheet, spun and knotted.

Present Tense

I know you are watching from some faraway voice,
and the sides of night are smashed by quiet.

—Michael Burkard

It's always dark when I picture you
now. You've turned off the lights
so you can see out better than we see in.

You're cataloging what you knew
in your life as a gifted kid,
and what you've learned since omniscience—

detailed notes about how we are living
and promises we've kept in our mundane,
to-do-list making, breathing lives.

It's expected that we, the grieving family,
would give your afterlife this hazy tint,
your spiral notebook edges frayed in the aftermath.

A boy discontent with his mind's tower,
a young man's body navigating the neighborhood
ocean with mild torment and a surfboard.

A Poem in Which You Become the Youngest in the Family

Ten days after my little brother's twenty-first birthday.
He is seventeen days older than you and we are remembering
the clammy air in the California hotel where we stayed
stoic-sad faces and ironed our shirts for your funeral.
I kept the key from that hotel
thinking it was a trip from which I'd need
a non-nightmare memento. Now we are all
older than you so there's a tension
between childhood memories—looking up
to you—and an impulse to counsel you
on life after college in hypothetical
unaddressable letters.

GUILT

Tonight, I hurt the feelings of a woman who liked me
when I missed the opportunity to keep my mouth shut—
and the laugh I expected from the seven people
around the table was replaced
by a quiet, smarter than me.

I don't know whether to send a note
of apology, or explanation, or to take this
second chance to shut up. I consider
sending cookies or a draft of this poem.

My condition is genetic.
Every Yom Kippur my mother and I lean
hard into each other as the synagogue repents
for the sin of gossip.

I'm tempted by strangers on the subway.
I consider telling the sweatered man next to me
that the trained gorilla in the book he's reading
is actually a lesbian in a gorilla costume—
so hurt by people she stopped being one.

R.H. Deadman Hospital

It is a specific spotlight of pain.
It is a torture session.
It is a celebration.
It is a wrestling match.
It is a sideshow.
It is red, always red, bright red.
It is the way her finger
would follow a shore bird,
pointing to a cormorant's
wings hitting the ocean
on takeoff.
It is the shadow left
by the largest tree
in all the acres she ever hiked
but without the comfort
of the woods, or consciousness.

Before I Get Out of Bed

I'm looking to replace
the two birds you killed with that stone
because I saw Ben Kingsley play Gandhi last night,
"an eye for an eye makes the whole world blind."
And, it's difficult to maneuver around
all those parakeet carcasses
after dreaming across a swinging rope bridge
made of thin planks and equivalent gaps.
Wavering above gaping wounds
made of quiet screams and masks.
It sure beats the dreams of a giant toilet
I must use in a crowd. Huge and hungry
vultures blinking pie-sized eyes at me.

One Head Stalking

I'm chewing the fleshy
insides of my lips and cheeks
thousands of miles away, in effigy.
A smoke outline of your days,
unsettled time in airports twirling a curl
around a reedy finger.

This morning I laid out the books
which molded you on the antique table
discretely. Mapping your universe
through finger-woven bindings
in a dusty apartment, running my dry palm
over the textured covers of your branching blueprints.

My hands curved around the spine and mouth
of a text that is not you,
and when I open the book,
thumbs skimming dulled corners,
I expect the book to sigh,
or creak, or whisper to me.

Rosie

My grandparents' house was a pointy brown triangle
with Grandpa Sam on the front step commanding:
Make, Rosie, Make
to the German Shepard who guided him down the sidewalk.
Rosie next to him, on the step, unharnessed
looking up at her master.

Rosie took her scraps directly from the table
but never mistook my grandmother's prosthetic arm,
lying around the house, for a chew toy.

Fanny and Sam were broken, like dolls
handled by careless children.
They were sharp cornered bricks,
dulled by separate cancers
in semi-private hospital rooms
before I learned to read.

Twenty-one years later,
on a New York train platform,
near the river where Fanny's champion-swimming sister
drowned saving a baby, I am listening
to families fight about the best route
and a green sweater and chicken bones.

A seeing-eye dog, a little smaller than Rosie,
stops directly in front of my seat on a black metal bench.
The man next to me quickly folds his newspaper,
leaps up to give his seat to the blind man.
But I do not move, the pen still in my hand,
I try to catch the dog's eye.

Rules of Poetry

You won't need to bring your dactyl to Trinidad.
They have one permanently affixed. Abu Dhabi,
population 347,000, is a double trochee whammy.
If everyone hates your work vehemently, isn't that a valid
emotional reaction? No surprise for the writer,
no surprise behind door number three there is never a car.

If your saddest day lasted three years, your manuscript
should take six. Never use a rose in a poem
unless it serves as a vehicle for death.
Find the ending of a phase, line, sarcophagus.
The grades don't mean anything. The rejections
make you squishier. These chains

are for your safety. Fasten them tightly about your
self. Dictate your dream journal to the winner
of the 1989 Brinker Elementary penmanship award.
Cull your subconscious for useable chunks and gasping.
Skin can bleed and our maps never fold neatly.
We would rather be famous after death.

Slippery Inside

THE MOUTH IS INTERESTING BECAUSE
IT'S ONE OF THOSE PLACES
WHERE THE DRY OUTSIDE MOVES
TOWARD THE SLIPPERY INSIDE

—JENNY HOLZER

The dry outside moves
toward the slippery inside,
a small spider traverses
a sleeping face
avoids the wind of nostrils
as dreams unwind each muscle
unclench every emotion, unpack
a man on the sidewalk who nods
morning as he scratches
his armpit as if to take you
somewhere borderline intimate,
carrying a newspaper
in a plastic sleeve that unwrapped
would leave an inky smudge
on a ballet dancer reading his first
review, to be clipped and mailed
in lick-sealed envelopes
to family hands that have wrung
with worry over a pair of feet
bent in satin slippers.

The dry outside moves
toward the slippery inside,
cheeks ache from inflating
every balloon to launch
in the schoolyard,
from children's hands,
peanut butter soft,
landing in overgrown lawns
free of childhood trappings.

The dry outside moves
toward the slippery inside,
your words come to me dripping
and I'm wringing out an entire year,
our hands cracked in winter,
small red lines that point
simultaneously toward
and away from our fears.

The Lobstermen's Daughters

Now the lobstermen invite their daughters
on the coldest wettest summer mornings
to help pull lobster pots,
from the seafloor, off the rocky coast,

on the coldest wettest summer mornings
we cannot learn how the smell
from the seafloor, off the rocky coast,
will stick to our skin for days,

we cannot learn how the smell—
salt-sky gray and sunrise,
will stick to our skin for days,
cormorants floating before the dive

salt-sky gray and sunrise
as fathers teach daughters complicated knots,
cormorants floating before the dive—
wings turn fins as they descend

as fathers teach daughters complicated knots
stay focused on the traps,
wings turn fins as they descend
feet beginning to freeze,

stay focused on the traps,
now the lobstermen invite their daughters,
feet beginning to freeze,
to help pull lobster pots.

ASPHALT

Plodding through the parking lot empty-chested
I'm wishing my car wasn't gray.
I'm wishing for a pinpoint of inspiration to propel me
through my list of goals penned at seventeen
in the end pages of my journal
along with lists of kisses and heroes,
both populated by too many white men.
Now I make nightly to-do lists.
Now I ponder the perfect bris gift
lifting each stuffed animal from the shelf
hugging it to find the four foot alligator
that cuddles best.

Bread from Many Ovens

My grandmother had hands
but no handwriting.
These are stock images in the closet
of the imaginary. In the drawers
that used to be card catalogs
with just enough numerals
to locate a book's incomplete index,
now you find a lifetime of clipped
fingernails or the pattern of dust
spiraling in the light between the blinds
in the bedroom your mother recovered
from childbirth, or a fever, or her own upbringing.
In the parent drawer the atmosphere is quick to anger.
At least you'd think so judging from the neon
parenting signs. I implore you—
make me invisible, or at least not subject to
the square dance rules of transition, not here,
not in the way the weather changes
every few minutes in non-California.
I always find an umbrella in the lost & found,
but it's the locket of hair that I'm seeking.
In her early old lady years my grandmother
dyed her hair the color of cheez. Orange lines
to the grade-skipping cousins. It was beautiful,
the way we didn't talk about death
until we learned to talk about it like rain.

Humid

Bleak visions of baseball games
where it's really hard to fall in love
with America, what with all
the sticky beer and cartoon mice
approaching on the street.
I remember when the wind
carried your scent back to me
after months where it just smelled humid
in the swamp and the skyscrapers
where I spend my days,
rubbing my head, hoping
friction will evoke heat
will evoke words will evoke
wings and suction cups.

Leave the Spine Behind

The moon was never made of shoelaces
but your spleen could very well
sneak out of your body at night
to follow its passion for origami, opera,
or rare meat. You probably wouldn't even notice
until someone at a bar punched you in the gut
and their knuckles found your vertebrae's grooves
and the message was sent from brain to tailbone
that to not have a hometown is a disadvantageous
situation to find yourself in when the family
roses are pulled from the ground.
They'll probably prescribe memorization
or thermonuclear meditation when the truth of the matter
is that anyway you position your bed in relation to the compass
destiny remains a crock of shit. The other crock is in the will
and it has never been a secret that the desire to end estrangement
wins three times out of seven. Statistics can prove the likelihood
of my knee finding your knee-pit in the middle of the night.
My scars are out of town at a storytelling convention
trying to coax a fervor from a haughty diphthong.

Crocus

Now in her forties,
living more than half her life
orphaned, she tried to tell a story
one hundred percent true.
It began with the exact color
of the sky that day.
The way the blue seemed
essentially dull. It's rare
to see that color
over the foothills
in springtime,
when the ground is made
mostly of mud.
Finally, it was the year when people
born the same year as her parents
began to die of natural causes.
Their dying felt a little delicious.

AUTOBIOGRAPHY

My blood is completely cheese.
If you peel back the layers
of this week's dreams a smart
fourth grader could tell you I feel
out of control of my life.
Cars drive themselves in opposition
of my steering instructions
until giant black bears set my car
down on the safe side of a mountain.
Plungers only make the problem wetter.
There are only four words in my
vocabulary, all adjectives.
I cannot describe the sound splash
down the wall of your childhood
bedroom. I cannot tie my shoe
by any non-bunny ear method.
I am straightforward or I sleep in.

Gag Reflex

I would prefer the ka-thunk of the phone
to be the only poem I wrote for you today.

I keep the memory of you somewhere near
my gag reflex, commingling with crumbs.

When someone has accidentally
entered my life wearing you, disguised

as fabric softener, the memory
floods down my throat, a liquid—not sweet—

coats my collarbones, spreads through my chest
to my armpits. That flavor of you

gropes its way down fleshy undersides of my arms,
to palms, curling, not clenched.

A Poem in Which the Word Casket Does Not Appear

Settling back into the dark
and the old brown couch
you tell me Bryn is dead.

The house carbon monoxided
her to sleep, hushed
lacey throws and antique thimbles.

How do you make
a death announcement
to an entire address book?

Numb young women
wail
closer and closer

to Bryn's body
refreshing their makeup
in jaunts to the toilet.

We should send kleenex
instead of cakes.

Mourners meet
in Massachusetts,
Manhattan, sweep up

grieving companions
along the way, embrace
down the coast.

The momentum of grief
pushes toward Virginia,
it tugs on cars and planes
recklessly, it
crumples little sisters.

Upon Receiving a Voicemail from the Person Who Most Recently Broke My Heart as Thomas Lux's Locks Run By

Today is warm enough
as long as you avoid the shade.
A short recording
of small talk waits for me,
logistical details,
the space between Philly and New York
and my favorite lighthouse in Maine
where I discovered my wrists
aren't the only wrists that smell beautiful
in the sunshine. Where lobstermen
take their daughters out
into the coldest, wettest summer
mornings. Now warming to the idea,
of returning the phone call
to the best case scenario.
I'm considering how to wrap up
my body again, sweaters
are folded and sniffed,
the idea of a new lover
wakes me up predawn.
I look at everybody's knuckles
and wish I were a sculptor
to cast my father's hands to scale
from when I rode on his shoulders
among the cherry blossoms and was lifted
up up crossing at dangerous intersections.
These days I'm examining
the hairstyles of poets
trying to gauge my place
between sensible and sexy
and the pull of the international
standard hair length.
The wind that blows your hair
between your lips or straight up
to commemorate
your one big idea.

Kidnapping Royalty

My poems are all about people I haven't seen in years
in casual contexts, looking like 1991, wearing vests
at summer camps and old apartments.

You are three years older than me
so I imagine we heard the same stories as children.

In your poems full of royalty, I assume
you're envisioning the characters from *Free To Be You and Me*
carrying scepters that thud a hollow sound on blacktop.
Their costumes won't win awards for precision,
believability, or even red and purple—or whatever
the royals are wearing to communicate
how difficult it is to live without want.

Your king and queen wouldn't be caught dead in my poem.
I'd have to hire the SLA to give up Uncle Lou,
our kidnapped family slumlord, and snatch their majesties
from separate canopied beds, where they sleep
in fits, unnaturally crooked to protect regal hairstyles
hiding their veins from the desire to cut the bloodline.

Kursk

Twenty-three underwater cosmonauts weep and sing at the deadly fireworks show. News comes that we're clinging to each other in complete darkness, while there's enough air to flex our cling muscles. We finger the lines on our faces in the blackness. We retrace the marks left by the extinct sun. We breathe apologies into the beaks of birds and send them back to the world. These kisses will arrive at the surface years in the future. They will make a slight splashing sound in the surf against a rock. The messages we had in our last moments will sound wet, *splish* or *woosh.*

The time it takes for a life to dissolve in saltwater and steel.

The Past

Our bodies are asymmetrical
long before our parents meet.
I only know one couple
whose secret relationship succeeded
once their socks were pulled up
to their knees and their collars
buttoned down. Back when
a scarf was a muffler
and power steering hadn't made us weak,
you could have more dirt
in your salad and less salad
in your life. It was much easier
to occupy your hands listening
to dramas and heroes and breakfasts
before tiny machines carpal-tunneled
our burgers bunless.

Jimmy Lee Tarpley

There is a certain type of man
happy only when working at summer camps.
We will call him The Counselor.
There's a way children look in a canoe
paddling into the distance of a machine-made lake
that affects the blood pressure, unless one looks
away and remembers something invigorating
from the morning news. The story need not
be about a moose freed from peril, but it's best
if the animal lover inside can radiate some frequency
pleasing to the neighborhood skunks
and encourage birds to shit
on someone else's car. If one drives a pickup
this message will get bounced around the bed
and come out in a non-animal-translatable form
of Flemish, especially American-made trucks.
The Counselor may win a local election
once his campers are of voting age. He can
instill confidence and the allure of a variety
of cold shower practical jokes. While most men
lose their fashion consciousness at age nineteen,
The Counselor always knows the latest
locker room styles. If he marries, the ceremony
will be decorated by both arts and crafts.
If he maintains a clandestine relationship
with the archery teacher all cupid metaphors
are off. Or the opposite may apply.

Hobby

I'm working on constructing a life
out of the pieces collected since Dallas's long expanse.
In Maine I found a tree curving into a woman
in the woods on an orange afternoon.
I left Cleveland with a single cold bulb
after the extinction of flash powder.
Austin gave me the minuet of bats
through streetlight's murmur.
I squeezed these into a thirteen-year-old hatchback
that died halfway to Chicago
where I found Harold Washington's ghost
and a lake so large it kept me
from having to look at Michigan.
Even his ghost was fairer than fair.

First Aid

When submitting to peer pressure
ignore any mature inclinations
listing the burn degrees.

First: submerge in a cool river
and follow with ice. Soothing beverages
may be poured over the ice, beware the porous.

Second degree: leave the identifying information
of your internet date with someone you trust.
Screen name alone is inadequate. Set a panic time.

Third degree: a high school physics teacher might
cite factual examples of spontaneous combustion
only the rubber soles remain. Char, smoke, poof.

The Red Cross warns: the saved
will sue in a litigious culture.
Clear the airway. Clear the airway.

If you can't spell tourniquet
don't bother coming to class.
Your skills are better suited to the surf.

When weaving a garment out of grass blades
remember to consult the pesticide schedule.
Eye wash of the damned. Eye wash organism.

A Poem in Which I Use Everyone's Real Name

The black woman who cuts
my mother's jewfro is named Bunny.
She's running late and the woman
with the next appointment is mean.
"Let it grow," Bunny advises.
This month my mother feels like a lion
just like Matt Rose who I cheated with
in high school computer science class.
Jon Reel, another computer scientist
I've made out with, worked for NASA
and cried in Houston on Charlie Fly's couch
after a sentimental science movie.
Tonight you frustrated me to tears
in some stubborn test of wills
and I was glad to have met some grown-ups
who respect my father, I remember
their Mississippi accents—but not their names.
Adam Simon wrote a play in which
a sexually transmitted disease
is named Jordan Klein after
the meanest kid in the class.
I hear that his little sister
Vanessa Klein is a single teen mother
and I try to remember what we ate
for snacks when I babysat her.
We slid in our socks to the kitchen
upsetting the dust bunnies gathered
in the corner with our wind-wake.

No Running at the Gene Pool

Reincarnation is a homeopathic antidote
for the biological clock.
My mother gave up on feeling
mature, before shelving the diaphragm.
Be cautious driving during leaf peeping season,
the mountain passes are rife
with tourists seeking that family smell.
Mine marches their way into poems
needing dandruff shampoo.
I eschew the river people
and the swell creeping toward their town.
My town baked and grew
and then all the restaurants changed
their menus, eliminating
the smoked-mozzarella-shrimp-quesadilla
a bona fide reason to visit.
You can never go home again.
At least you can't order the same thing.
You also can't go back to summer camp
because once you get hairy they're altogether
uninterested. Wildflowers grow
out of cow pies, but Texas state law
prohibits my ninth grade biology project.
If you got up early enough
the Jewban teacher did a lesson
on bananas and prophylactics
but the Christian Coalition arrived
by second period to meet teens at the pole.
We were educated halfway between
American made and de-boned carp.
The variety that swims to find its place
between the parking lot's yellow lines.
I'll articulate embarrassing details
in my best script, when it comes out of my mouth
the curls will cumulonimbize around
mourner's heads, protected by black lace hats.

BOUNDARIES

There's a line on a map that separates
ah-mens from aye-mens—
there is a geography of faith.

Zealots whirl poisonous snakes
in foothills and homes
in celebration of what's green.

The line of the snake circles,
a wheel expels treachery,
a holywall alienates and crumbles.

There is a line on your asymmetrical
face where they sewed your ear
back to your head. I study it

while you are sleeping,
your torso draws a dented line
in the mattress, a line I've traced,
the length of you, hallelujah!

In an Emergency

I remember the exact moment
my father taught me how to spit,
toothpaste rarely dribbled on my chin
after he said the words *pucker*
and *push* three years before I sobbed
to our out-of-town guest
that there is no 9-1-1 service
for a home so rural,
as dad had a heart attack, wordless
on the kitchen floor.

I remember a woman who was almost
my mother explaining
that it helps to think
what you are going to say
before you actually say it.
I think about funerals more
than my wedding dress.

I will always have an escape plan,
a suitcase packed with my most valuable
photos and charms, its handle pointed up
in case of fire. The emergency number
is written on the phone, even in the metropolis
I've chosen, even though it is 9-1-1,
even here, two blocks from the hospital,
sixteen years and a thousand miles later.

Juniper Point, Maine

I'm seven years of brain cells away
from your family's delicate plumbing system
and glacier of dirty paper plates.

I haven't met a talking-vodka-filled watermelon
since you told me about the swim to impress
your thirteen-year-old girllove
which led to hypothermia/asthma/
unreturned notes taped to the bulletin board
where a mailboxless town picks up their mail.

My mail has been worse
since that summer. I hoped that
by sending a box of twinkies
you'd remember to remember me.

I hoped I could always drive fast on island roads
in an imitation of a local or someone at least
who has a home. I never wore that shirt
to be confused with a lobsterman
and I never expect the job title to coax daughters
onto the boats. I'll be on the dock
protecting my mother's crabmelt from the gulls.

Terminus Adolescent

His name is William Williams,
does that bother anyone else?
What are the repercussions
of irresponsible naming? I mean,
if you don't become the punisher.
This new toddler model is entirely
reprogrammable. These kids
haven't seen that Ghoulies commercial
that implores kids to wet their beds.
Their ketchup is green.
I handed a fat lost beagle to one.
She took the pooch around to homes
in the tudor tradition. Weeks later
I saw a lost beagle poster three states away
and made a mental note
to not ask for directions.
What bad marketing that Snoopy is.
What a palace, but where's the moat?
When the pillow smells of the sea
and you are land locked
your dreams will inevitably
take you to the garden state.
I've been there quietly celebrating Bastille Day.
I've dreamt the slow deaths.
It's always cold when I wake,
the blankets collecting individual dog hairs
pooled around the bedlegs.
In this climate I can get away
without nighttime woolens.
The cicada molt their three dee melody,
my legs are frictionless.
A greased pig walks into a bar.
Beer drinkers can never find
the bottle cap receptacle
in time to circumvent the storm
through the countertops.
It's the same. Two eyes, one nose
and a suspicion of incomparable genius—
according, at least, to first grade
standardized tests in the fire-
proof safe.

Lake Placid

I panted all the way up the steep trail
that proved you're in better shape than me,
appreciating your balance and talent
in not sending any rocks rolling,
branches snapping back.
The pond at the top was so much like
one you'd find on a Manhattan dentist's wall
to calm the patient and distract from
the poking and scraping and picking.
I was not calm, didn't trust the lake would allow you
to swim across, amidst its bullfrog tadpoles.
I was in the dentist's chair watching your long armstrokes and their
wake in the water, wondering what the ripple effect
of the gasses looked like in my lungs,
breathing a deep metronome
to accompany Dr. Watters's murmurs.
Is there anything I can breathe
so the muscles connecting my shoulders
to my chin will relax for the entire
eight-hour drive to your childhood
home? A place full of active and passive deer
and a recurring mammal that looks like
a mutant miniature beaver.
I could call it gopher or muskrat
or Ezmerelda the Amazing
and buy her some kind of rodent outfit
in colors inspired by the umbrella
I remember I've left in the car
at the exact moment of the first serious
thunderclap. I calculate the distance
one wet human can travel in a downpour
while protecting precious antique paper dolls.

Absolutely Nothing

Poetry has to be this:
A girl in a wheatfield—
Or its absolutely nothing.

—Nicanor Parra

I've expelled the girl from the wheatfield,
handed her this knapsack and sent her to the shrines of the alphabet.
No more grass between her toes, brown bottomed feet, calluses.
After all those years of wheat she'll be ready for the card catalog.
I've built a whole and unwavering wall between the girl
and her wheatfield, not nearly as unpoetic as a movie
about a baseball field amidst a cornfield.
That was a story about fathers; this is a metaphor for cotton dresses.
A girl leaving the field forever.
Sure, some non-stalk portion of the wheat
might get stuck to her heel, or show up years later
when she's looking through a crate to find the scarf
a now wheatfield-less girl could wear to the opera.
One kernel wedged between the golden landscape
of sun, wheat, husks, and the black elbow-length gloves.

I'M FROM TEXAS BUT I'M NO COWBOY-POET

If you live near the Oklahoma border,
your horse is old and frail,
but you don't have the heart to send it
to the metaphorical glue factory,
you can donate it to that non-profit
summer camp for diabetic kids
on the edge of Lake Dealey.

I rode those horses: Bullet and Fireball,
Rainbow and Brownie,
sweating on the red dirt trails
at one hundred and six degrees.
A well-trained counselor in front
and another packed with medical supplies
in the rear of our sluggish drive.

At camp I first met small-town Texas,
George Strait, Garth Brooks and learned
the Texas Two-Step with a dreamy
Jewish medical student name Spark.
We'd dance, monkey scream,
or talk about my discomfort at *chapel*
where they said *nondenominational*
and meant just plain *Christian.*

Island Life

It is the best kind of fame for me,
a quiet small-town fame in a town
where the library hours are not posted
but signified by the tomato-shaped
minivan the librarian parks
in front of the shoebox library,
while she tends the town's
quiet gossip and the twenty-five cent
paperbacks bequeathed by an island couple
who sat on their porch reading
through a fifty-year marriage
where they didn't mind the water being too cold,
or the beaches made of precarious rocks.
They used postcards from their grown children
as bookmarks, short sentences
of a relaxing vacation in the desert or
reaching the west coast in 1963,
they were addicted to westerns, romances,
and the sea air that compromised their spines.

Liquidation Sale

You will reach a lifepoint
when the pictured collars
of thirty years ago
evoke a warm ketchup feeling, not a
what were they thinking? electrode.

We're all dying, all pulling
our laces so tight, later
you will have red line evidence
on your bare feet
sliding under the untucked.

In Olympic diving the goal
is to make a splash much smaller
than my olive propelled
from toothpick to gin.
Ties are just stain magnets afterall.

Every seven years you have
an entirely new body.
Each cell free of the crap
of shitty 1998. In nine years
you'll have the same bad habits.

Around age thirty
you'll talk freely about
your STD history.
If you have kids you'll talk
poo and movie ratings.

Who do you have to know
to die painlessly in your sleep?
Rumor has it the afterlife menu
is bland, go ahead
ride the motorcycle.

Arthritis, shingles, eyelash curler,
hemorrhoids, hair loss, hangnail
depilatory, puberty, osteoporosis,
mowing the lawn, short-term,
long-term memory loss.

Everything
must
go.

Transportation Dream #2

my parents carry the smell of coffee
from breakfast table
to the world of the airless;
wisps of lake algae,
underwater skyscrapers
bend in our train's wake—

we are safe from their menace
in this city just below our city;
gripping our melting sticks of gum,
wondering why all horror films aren't underwater,
non-tropical fish dance a lethargic swagger
in this terrible botanical garden

lacking the cherry-red flavor
of our landlives, which we've left
for these cobalts and brown;
pupils grow despite our attempts
to remember the turquoise glimpse
of surface-light and the smell of the forest

The Windshield Factory

The unintended byproducts of the windshield factory
make it cold enough to freeze Molly's nose hairs crispy.
"Welcome to Maine!" it announces, "I'll teach you how to layer."

On the outside we wear a less perfect version
of the plans our parents made after the midwife left the room.

Between that and our magma, we've piled on
the bad haircuts and glasses, that were pink or red or blue
and took up a geographically significant portion of face.

All this external stuff can itch.
It never actually touches the skin.

Flimsily placed next in line are life's unwritten liner notes.
The scene from high school where someone illustrated tact
and drew the frontier between the two of you.

The day the babysitter's dad died and you rushed to the hospital
in her too-small-to-be-safe car. My father was taken to that hospital
thirteen years later, with a concussion reminiscent of Pam.

You can survive in near-freezing water
for the minutes your body keeps blood
in your organs and sacrifices your soccer career.

In the part of you that's always cooking there are
organic potholders to protect you from the prickly pear.

The Textures of Concealing

This is the heavy piece of velvet I've
strung across troublesome emotion.

It's class warfare, the way cashmere feels
rubbing up against you on the subway.

I've never had a good cry, despite my
recent commitment to folding Kleenex.

Holding a styrofoam coffee cup out
to the homeless does not save the village.

Such difficulty, to compress raging
feelings onto simple cardboard signs.

Does wool make you itch, Rachel? It's Tuesday,
three above zero, and this is your life.

Notes

"Condor Man" is for Kimberly Ann Grossman Conception and Linda Isaacson.

"Knotty" is for Zdena Heller.

Nixzmary Brown, a Brooklyn seven-year-old, died as a result of abuse and neglect on January 10, 2006. Her mother and stepfather were charged with murder.

"Crocus" is for Tara J. Pearson.

"A Poem in Which the Word Casket Does Not Appear" is dedicated to Bryn Parry.

"Kidnapping Royalty" is for Matthea Harvey.

The Kursk is a Russian submarine that sank in August of 2000.

"Hobby": Harold Washington was the first black mayor of Chicago. He served from April 29, 1983 until November 1987. He died in office after being elected to a second term.

"No Running at the Gene Pool": A Jewban is a Cuban Jew.

"Terminus Adolescent" thanks Stereolab for their song title.

"Lake Placid" is for Karen.

ACKNOWLEDGMENTS

The author would like to thank the publications where the poems from this collection first appeared:

Black Rock & Sage: "Bread from Many Ovens"
Can We Have Our Ball Back?: "Edibles," "Autobiography," and "First Aid"
Forklift, Ohio: "Before I Get Out of Bed" and "&"
Fugue: "Windshield Factory" which also was a finalist for the 2005 Fugue Poery Prize
88: "Improvisation," and "Leave the Spine Behind"
H_ngm_n: "Liquidation Sale" and "When You're Not Allowed to Daydream"
Incliner: "Recipe for Success"
Lumina: "Upon Receiving a Voicemail From the Person Who Most Recently Broke My Heart" and "Rosie"
North American Review: "Rules of Poetry" which also was a finalist for the James Hearst Poetry Prize
Poetry Magazine: "Improvisation"
Small Spiral Notebook: "Kursk," "No Running at the Gene Pool," and "The Past"
Southern Poetry Review: "Boundaries"

"Improvisation" was also reprinted in *Real Sofistkashun: Essays on Poetry and Craft* by Tony Hoagland (Graywolf Press, 2006).